GOD'S VERY GOOD DESIGN

Equipping parents with God's word for foundational conversations about sex.

Copyright © 2012 by Mary Flo Ridley
Published by Mary Flo Ridley
All rights reserved.
Printed in the United States of America.

Scripture quotations are from The Holy Bible, English Standard Version (ESV)
Copyright © 2001 by Crossway Bibles, a publishing ministry of Good News
Publishers.
Used by permission.
All rights reserved.

ISBN 978-0-9858317-0-7

www.maryflo.org

DEDICATION

This book is dedicated to the young parents for whom it was written—To those who want a new way to navigate these waters in a way that honors God and gives light and life to their children. I pray His blessing on you and your children.

"Great is the LORD, and greatly to be praised, and His greatness is unsearchable. One generation shall commend your works to another, and shall declare your mighty acts." Psalm 145:3-4

A NOTE OF GRATITUDE

To Dave, Meg & Travis, Jill & Ryan, and Davis...Oh the JOY of being the wife and mother of the Ridley family! Not only are you my family, you are my favorite people in the world. Could we please go back and do it all over again?

To Ann Higginbottom...Thank you for being my writing partner, my chief of staff, my new dear friend, and the word-artist for this book. I am humbled by your dedication and devotion, appreciating that you shared your God-given talent with me and with these parents. This book would not be here without your steady and smiling presence. You are another reminder to me that God hears us when we pray!

To Natalie Wills, our graphic artist, and our budding artists whose beautiful work graces these pages.

To the voices of encouragement, who spurred me on to continue this work...Your timely words and prayers meant more than you will ever know. I want to especially thank: Daddy, Buck, Debbie, Melissa, Carroll, Elizabeth, Brad, Minerva, Linda, Susan, Patrick, Dan, Anna, Melissa, Alan, Jill, Meredith, Julie, Laura, Michele, Leslie, Nancy, Becky, Nell, Susan, Christy, Kay, Lori, Kari, Laurie, Just Say YES, the Council for Life, and the Table Group...but above all, Dave and the kids.

FORWARD

By Nell F. Bush, Ph. D.

The book that you hold in your hands will be a marvelous blessing to you and your family. I know from first hand experience as a mom of four that the Lord uses Mary Flo's curriculum in great ways. Her approach to the sensitive and complex issue of human sexuality is highly professional and informative, but also wonderfully humorous and comforting. She helps parents feel completely at ease, as well as empowered to share important truths and values with their children.

As a Child Development Specialist, I speak to a variety of parenting groups throughout North Texas. My focus is typically on developmental and discipline-related issues, but invariably I receive numerous questions on teaching children about sex. I consistently refer to Mary Flo's program and now look forward to recommending this fantastic book as a resource. I am so thankful to have this model as a reference point because parents always find it extremely helpful.

As a mom, my own family has benefited tremendously from Mary Flo's teaching. My husband and I have closely followed her protocol with all four of our children. As a result, our children view us as the "experts" on sexual matters and have felt free to ask us questions through the years. We clearly see how this has strengthened our parent-child bond and has been a great gift to our children.

I couldn't imagine a better way to shape our thoughts about sexuality as parents. This book is not only a delightful read, but it is informative and helpful like a textbook. Mary Flo is passionate about her convictions and is charming and approachable at the same time. I am blessed to know her as a colleague and friend. My hope is that more and more families will have the opportunity to be encouraged by her positive message through ***God's Very Good Design.***

REAL THOUGHTS from REAL PARENTS

Moms and Dads...
Sometimes it is helpful to hear from other parents, just like you. I invited some parents to offer feedback about content you will find in this book. When asked, "What was most helpful?" this is what they had to say:

> *"Breaking down the 'sex talk' into easy and biblical truths was so informative & entertaining. You made it easier than I was making it!"*

"I was so grateful to have the step by step process for all of the conversation. I love how Mary Flo broke it down into stages. What a blessing! Thank you for giving us the words to use and then empowering us to use them."

> *"As a former health educator, I know how much kids need to hear this. I wish all parents would incorporate this in their homes."*

"It is wonderful to learn how to deliver our beliefs in God's plan to our children without embarrassment—thank you!"

"I knew that it was important to talk with my children early and now I have a strategy."

> *"This content gave me some great tools to get started along with the awareness that I do need to get started. Beginning the conversation early is the way to build a comfort level and form a plan. It is helpful to be strategic."*

"I love the idea of filling our kids with good & godly information first! I realize that protecting my child from the topic of sex is not the best approach. Mary Flo offers a reasonable, viable, values-based, and proactive game plan."

> *"I now understand that 'the sex talk' is not one big conversation. Rather, it comes in little conversations along the way. We received a very doable, repeatable strategy for addressing and shaping our children's sexual character."*

"We love the simple conversation tips for explaining birth, reproduction and conception. They are practical and biblical. I now feel ready and confident to talk to my seven-year-old son. In the past I have ignored or dodged his questions when he was ready to talk. Now I know what to say."

CONTENTS

Preface 12

Introduction 14

Step One: Message 23
Creating a godly message of sex for your children

Step Two: Vocabulary 37
Defining male and female according to God's design

Step Three: Birth 49
Explaining God's miracle of birth

Step Four: Reproduction 59
Exploring God's design in all of creation

Step Five: Conception 71
Revealing the oneness and fruitfulness of God's design for marriage

Parting Thoughts 85

Cheat Sheet 88

About Mary Flo Ridley 91

PREFACE

The Lord's work through this ministry started a long time ago. It has been a privilege to be a part of it. In 1986 I began conducting workshops for parents with the goal of teaching them how to shape their child's sexual character through early conversations. I encouraged them to spark these conversations while their children were young, preferably in the preschool to early elementary ages. The simple steps that I outlined in those workshops followed a natural pattern of a child's development and curiosity.

However, the Lord had something more in store for this ministry. As a believer in God's word, I wanted to connect the dots between these simple steps and His infallible word. The dream for this book came from my desire to share with parents the scriptures that I find foundational for conversations about sexuality.

The dawning of your child's understanding about sex actually begins with your own understanding and in your early commitment to teach your children. Near the beginning of your child's life you have opportunities to make impressions that are both subtle and deep. Fortunately for us, God gives us all that we need right at the beginning of His word. In the book of Genesis, God begins to unfold what He wants us to know about life, and this is a good place for us to begin as well.

Amazingly, the simple steps that I have shared with parents in workshops and His word follow the same order. For many years I have encouraged parents to unfold the conversations that introduce sex in this order:

1) Parent's message
2) Vocabulary
3) Birth
4) Reproduction
5) Conception

In God's word, we see a parallel pattern:
1) Creating an image (Gen. 1:26)
2) Creating humans: male & female (Gen. 1:26)
3) Multiplying to new generations (Gen. 1:28)
4) The use of seeds for reproduction of all living things (Gen. 1:29)
5) The beauty of marital oneness (Gen. 2:24)

It is fascinating to notice the very same order. God is the designer of good things. Together let's look and see what He has called His very good design.

INTRODUCTION

THE JOYS OF CHILDHOOD

Sometimes a beach chair gives us the best view for the sweetest moments of parenthood. Imagine that's where you are right now. Your toes are tucked in the sand and the ocean is close enough that you can catch its mist with each new wave. Everything around you echoes God's goodness and brilliance in creation. You have the sand beneath your feet and the birds soaring overhead, yet nothing captures your attention like the beauty and joy that dances before you: your children, enjoying a day at the beach. They run and skip and squeal, tracing the lingering line of the surf in the midst of a playful game of chase. A sandpiper scurries just inches ahead of the spirited pursuit. Only the distraction of a burrowing crab redirects the kids' attention. Kneeling down into the shallow tide pool, their little fingers get right to work as they dig frantically to keep up with the crab's path of escape. Their laughter reminds you of how sweet it is to be a mom or a dad.

In that moment, life seems so simple. Your little family, enjoying a simple day and the simple joy of just being together. Those are the moments that parents frame in their minds. Simple innocence—if only time could stand still! Parenthood is filled with these simple joys, but there are days when life doesn't seem like "a day at the beach." Those precious, curious minds grow in their fascination with the world around them. Sometimes their questions dance around topics that are easy to tackle. "Why can't fish live out of the water? What is lightning? How long will it take me to dig a hole to the other side of the world?" But other times, their inquiries make even Mom and Dad begin to squirm a bit!

Childhood is such a sweet time of innocence. Why would anyone interrupt the play and comfort of "being a kid" with information that makes everyone uncomfortable? But sooner or later, you will begin to hear questions like, "How does a baby get out of a mommy?" Or even a harder question like, "How did that baby get in there?" These are questions that some of us would like to defer to a later time, but what if this moment of curiosity is exactly the right time to meet children where they are? It's easy to rest in the old saying that "ignorance is bliss" when it comes to our children. But the years of your children being children are also incredibly important. Foundations that are laid in the early years will have a great impact on the growing years of your family. Let's take steps together towards laying a firm foundation.

AND SO WE BEGIN!

I know what you may be thinking. Conversations about sexuality sound intimidating, uncomfortable and at times, completely overwhelming. But guess what? They don't have to be. Early conversations answering those tricky questions about birth and conception will begin the journey of your conversations about sex. **Let's consider this question together: how and when will you begin conversations with your children about sex?** The book that you are holding in your hands is designed to help answer that question. Parents often go to the most complicated parts of the conversations with their children about sex, but we want to take it back to the basics. Think "simple." A simple book with a simple plan that gives you simple steps to follow. This is a book that walks with you as you point your children to God's very good design. Have you ever thought about sex that way? God's very good design. That's a beautiful place to begin.

Perhaps you're holding this book and feeling overwhelmed. Don't be! Talking to your children about sexuality is a big deal, but we can tackle the topic with small steps. Thankfully, our babies don't come into the world already walking and running. There is a progression: sitting up, crawling, scooting, first steps and then walking. I hope you will see conversations about sex in a similar manner. Through a variety of age appropriate conversations, you have the privilege of unfolding the beauty and mystery that is God's gift of sex to His people, one step at a time.

Our default is to do what our parents did. This is a natural progression, unless you are intentional about being different. Grandmother's apple pie will always taste the same until someone changes the recipe. We learn so much from our parents and the way they raised us. There is great beauty in tradition, but I'd like to invite you to consider the ways that changing things up can be a really good and healthy thing for a family. Perhaps the topic of sex was taboo in your family growing up. What if that were different in your family today? What would that look like? Sometimes "different" is a really good thing!

"Now wait, Mary Flo. Shouldn't I wait until they are older?" That's a great question. Yes of course, some aspects of sexuality—like the dangers and pleasures—are best saved until your children are mature enough to handle them. But remember, we are hoping for a strong foundation. God's very good design is a great place to begin. Little minds are curious—don't you agree? Tiny questions are opportunities to lay that first brick of the foundation. Capture the teachable moments. Imagine that you can see the long and winding river of your child's life. Now look down the river a little bit. What can you do today that will impact the journey ahead?

A little word of warning as we begin to talk about sex with our children: the culture is relentless in sharing its perspectives. Our children are inundated with confusing ideas about sexuality that come from television, movies, music, magazines and the internet. Culture is yelling, and the culture's voice will be the only voice that your children hear UNLESS you speak up. Ideally your voice will be the one that makes the first impression on your children. Let's find our voice together.

WHAT DOES GOD'S WORD SAY?

My prayer is that, as parents, we would begin and end with our feet planted in God's word. I can't think of a more secure place to begin this journey. Interestingly, God does not shy away from addressing the topic of sexuality. In fact, He mentions it right in the beginning! This must be important! At the very beginning of God's word, Genesis opens wide the door of talking about sexuality. Before we go any further, let's consider what the Bible says:

"Then God said, 'Let us make man in our image, after our likeness…' So God created man in his own image, in the image of God he created him; male and female he created them.

And God blessed them. And God said to them, 'Be fruitful and multiply and fill the earth and subdue it, and have dominion over the fish of the sea and over the birds of the heavens and over every living thing that moves on the earth.' And God said, 'Behold, I have given you every plant yielding seed that is on the face of all the earth, and every tree with seed in its fruit. You shall have them for food.'" Genesis 1:26-29

"Therefore a man shall leave his father and his mother and hold fast to his wife, and they shall become one flesh. And the man and his wife were both naked and were not ashamed." Genesis 2:24-25

God's word shows us that there is a beautiful, perfect order to follow for our simple plan of talking to our children about sex. God has already done the work for us in His word, teaching us plainly about His intentions for His creation. So, let's begin where God's word begins. That makes a lot of sense to me.

FIVE SIMPLE STEPS

One of my favorite parts of being a mom is holding onto those precious, chubby hands. You know what I'm talking about. A little fist fits perfectly in the palm of your hand. Think about holding that sweet, little hand as you go for a walk down the street or even through a crowded mall. There is something really dear and significant about those tiny hands. Imagine the five chubby fingers that busy themselves throughout the day—painting, playing, digging and eating. For each little finger, let's think about five simple steps for this book.

Let me begin by reminding you to consider the uniqueness of your family. Chances are, your family won't look like the Ridley family or any other family.

That's part of the beauty of God's design! Using God's word in Genesis as our map, I have developed a simple strategy that aims at helping you begin conversations with your children. I pray that these steps will invite you to consider how you might apply them to your unique and special family. It's really quite simple:

STEP ONE: Your **Message**—Creating a godly message of sex for your children

STEP TWO: Respectful **Vocabulary**—Defining male and female according to God's design

STEP THREE: Story of **Birth**—Explaining God's miracle of birth

STEP FOUR: Design of **Reproduction**—Exploring God's design in all of creation

STEP FIVE: Story of **Conception**—Revealing the oneness and fruitfulness of God's design for marriage

Together, we will walk through each step, directed by God's good and perfect word. And just like a baby learning to walk, we will take it one step at a time.

MY HOPE

I have many hopes for this book. In my first book *Simple Truths with Mary Flo Ridley*, I gave parents a parenting strategy for approaching this topic, but it lacked a biblical grid. In this book, I hope to expand on that strategy by giving it a biblical context and foundation. First let me offer an open invitation to all types of parents. Parenting looks different all around the world. Whatever your parenting situation: husband/wife team, single parent, adoptive parent or teen parent: WELCOME! I'm so glad that you are here. It doesn't matter what your situation looks like: God's very good design has you perfectly placed as the parent of your sweet children.

This book is coming from a mom who didn't do it perfectly. My husband Dave and I have three grown children (two girls and a boy) and we certainly have learned plenty along the way! I hope you will join me as a parent who longs to see her children grow in wisdom and stature, in favor with God and man (Luke 2:52). Through my journey, I have learned the importance of focusing on relationships, maintaining open lines of communication, and being approachable. I hope we can grow in these areas together.

This book is the culmination of so many thoughts and prayers. In short, I have three hopes for my message:

HELPFUL. As a parent myself, I know where you are coming from! And I long to help. I hope that this book will help you to find your voice and equip you with words to speak. Sometimes we just need a little help getting started.

SIMPLE. I really hope that you find this book to be simple - a quick read when your house is quiet during naptime. Parenting often means that our personal time flies out the window. But I hope the simplicity of this book makes you feel like you can pick it up when the dust settles, even if it's only between the moments of a nap and a snack.

GOD-GLORIFYING. I hope this book points you to God's word. No other book paints such a perfect picture of His very good design. So if you don't remember a single thing I say, I pray you will remember God's word.

Will you join me? It really is an exciting journey learning to parent our precious children towards God's intended plan. Let's start out together—seeing the beauty of God's design in the midst of the battle of this world. At the end of it all, I am certain we will see a clearer picture of God's redeeming grace.

STEP ONE

CREATING A GODLY MESSAGE OF SEX FOR YOUR CHILDREN

"Let us make man in our image, after our likeness." Genesis 1:26

FIRST: A VERY GOOD PLAN

If you take a long look at creation, you will notice a particular, beautiful order to things. Whether you are marveling at a flower or you are surrounded by a mountainous landscape, creation echoes with reminders of a good and perfect plan. To stand before the mighty ocean or under the canopy of an infinite night sky, it seems impossible to miss the visible hand of a mighty Creator—who had a masterful plan. Every detail is so intricately laid out. Creation points to a creative God with a perfect plan. And above everything that He created, God ended with a triumphant finale—man and woman, made in His image.

God was very intentional in His design. Therefore, we ought to be intentional in the messages we send our children, and the image that those messages create. Before God created man, He had a grand plan for His creation. Before the weaving and spinning of man in His image, the Lord knew exactly what He envisioned. He planned it. And then He made it. Let's look together at the beginning of God's Word:

"Then God said, 'Let us make man in our image, after our likeness' … So God created man in his own image, in the image of God he created him; male and female he created them. And God saw everything that he had made, and behold, it was very good. And there was evening and there was morning, the sixth day." Genesis 1:26-27, 31

After all of creation—the crawling animals, the flying birds, the peaks and the valleys—God made humans. And He made them specifically male and female, detailed in His own image. God made us to reflect His glory and character in the world. Made in His image, we were the pinnacle of all creation. The Lord stood back and examined His handiwork. He saw that everything He made was beyond "good," it was "very good." That includes you and me—the very good exclamation marks of creation. God had a plan and then He took action. What a perfect example to follow.

TAKING THE FIRST STEP: HAVE A PLAN

Imagine baking a cake for your child's birthday party. Your kitchen is brimming with all sorts of ingredients, spices and essentials. And yet you wouldn't dare put on a blindfold and toss things into a bowl. You need a strategy. You need a recipe. Just like a game plan is essential to any game, a recipe is necessary to create a tasty dessert. With the plan in place, baking is full of purpose. I'd love for us to consider a similar method when it comes to talking to our children about sex.

Conversation with your children begins only after you do some work behind the scenes. Once you have a plan, the actual conversations become less daunting and seem filled with greater purpose. Before you talk with your children, I invite you to begin the conversation with each other. Just as parenting looks different from family to family, so will these conversations.

Moms and dads who are parenting together, it is so important for you to learn how to talk with each other. For single parents, I would encourage you to take time to think and pray about what your vision will be for your child. Regardless of your parenting situation, the goal is the same: turn to God in His Word and in prayer so that you might grow a vision for godly sexuality that you wish to impart to your children. As you seek this goal, you will have all that you need for the task of talking to your children. Perhaps this step seems like a simple one. But of all the steps we will take together, it is the most essential and critical. Creating a message means that we are striving towards something that holds more weight than words. **What is the overall message your family will have about sex?**

Together with your spouse or even in the quiet thoughts of your journal and prayers, begin to think about and talk about your view of sex. Consider what you were taught about sex and how you view it today. A good place to begin is talking about your current perspective and your perspective as a child. As you begin to explore your own thoughts—past and present—you will begin to shape a hope for your child's future. Sometimes, the best place to begin is with asking a good question.

LEARNING TO ASK QUESTIONS

A tremendous blessing to any relationship is the ability to ask good, open-ended questions, the kind of questions that invite relationship and more dialogue. Talk to your spouse. Ask questions of yourself. A good way to start thinking about your vision and message is to do a little digging, discovering what is most important to you when it comes to talking about sex.

> **The work of creating an image or vision is foundational to the whole process.**

Begin asking yourself and/or your spouse questions that pertain to you and also to your children. The work of creating an image or vision is foundational to the whole process. This first step will affect everything else we desire to accomplish. So it is important that we give it proper time and attention. There is an endless list of questions that could be beneficial along the way, but here are a few that might help you get started:

> *What would you say is the purpose of sex?*
> *What is the role of sex within marriage?*
> *Describe our culture's view of sex. How is it different from your view?*
> *How did you first learn about sex? Was it a positive or negative experience? Why?*
> *How did that first exposure affect your thinking or behavior?*
> *What was the attitude about sex in your home of origin?*
> *What decisions did you make about your own sexual activity?*
> *Are there any decisions you regret? Are there some you hope your children also make?*
> *Has your image of sex changed through the years?*
> *Has there been any abuse or destructive behavior that needs to be addressed?*

Whether your life has been filled with joy or hurt—or most likely a mixture of both—it is important to realize that there is great purpose in your past. Your past does not define you, but it does contribute to how you think about the future. That is why it is essential that we start in this very important place. However our past has shaped our sexual character, we need to know that God is in the business of redemption—making all things new. Some will have a story of naïveté. Others have made a lot of sexual mistakes. Let's start from the place of remembering together that the Lord brings beauty out of ashes. He covers our past and gives us new hope for the future. The gospel changes everything because we have new life in Christ!

It is an important work to consider your past experiences and how they shape your understanding of sex. In a marriage, it is essential to discuss these details with your spouse. Even uncomfortable and difficult conversations will be a blessing to this process and to your marriage.

In His work of redemption, the Lord has a way of making the past and future collide. The consideration of your past opens a wide avenue to think and pray about your child's future. As we begin to dream about that future, we move through the process of reconciliation with our past. While it may be easier said than done, making peace with your past is an integral part of creating a positive legacy for your children. As a parent, I invite you to learn from your past and then move forward towards a positive future for your growing family.

DREAMING ABOUT THE FUTURE

It is an exciting process to dream about your children's future. Perhaps you dream about their career or even the impact that they will have on the world. From the moment your baby is born, I am sure you were filled with hopes and dreams for the life ahead. In those dreams, do you ever think about their sexual character? As we continue in conversations, it is helpful to have some questions to consider:

What do you hope your children will learn about sex?
What will be your intended attitude towards sex in your home?
What do you hope your children's first impression of sex will be?
What is the main idea that you hope to convey in your conversations?
What choices do you hope they will make in the future?
Imagine your child married. What do you hope this will be like for them?

How do you want your child's understanding of sex to be different from your early understanding?

It was always helpful for me to remember that we are not merely fighting against something (the confusing ideas of the current culture). We are fighting FOR something. If we are fighting FOR a positive and God-honoring vision of sexuality, the things we are fighting against will seem less intimidating. As parents, we must have something we are fighting towards. When it comes to your children's sexuality, what is the positive side of the fight? As loving parents, I know that you are doing everything in your power to protect your children from the demeaning messages of the Internet or TV. But a strategy that is only defensive is simply not enough. We must also engage in an offensive battle, relaying a positive message to our children. There is a message of beauty within strong boundaries.

A visual image is sometimes helpful. As we were able, my husband Dave and I welcomed opportunities to teach our children about marriage. Taking them to weddings and showing them pictures from our wedding, we tried to paint a picture for our children. When you give your family something to fight FOR, the battle against culture will seem less oppressive. Paint a picture of the vision for your children. What do you want them to see?

GOD'S WORD IS CRUCIAL

Now you have considered your past and your children's future. These steps are key, but they are not the most important things to consider as you develop an image or vision. Understanding what God's word says about sexuality is crucial. Think about your core beliefs and values. Where do you get them? Are they based on human wisdom or on God's revelation? Do people decide the purpose of sex or has God already done so?

In thinking about your message and overall vision, nothing is more important than looking to God's word for direction. There is beautiful clarity in its message. The world gives us a ton of confusing messages about sex. We desperately need clarity! But to be clear with our children, we ourselves must be clear. Together, let's look to the Designer to understand His very good design.

"How can a young man keep his way pure? By guarding it according to your word." Psalm 119:9

Living according to God's word offers guidance to our steps. In a quest for purity, making our steps according to His word brings careful boundaries to our lives.

"I call heaven and earth to witness against you today, that I have set before you life and death, blessing and curse. Therefore choose life, that you and your offspring may live, loving the LORD your God, obeying his voice and holding fast to him, for he is your life and length of days." Deuteronomy 30:19-20

Our sovereign God has set before us the choice of life and death. Our culture has a way of offering us things that look like life, but really bring us harm in the end. Death pretends to be life. Sex can easily fall into this category of confusion. God's word is clear: choose life—life in Christ with boundaries that are blessings.

"Brothers, I do not consider that I have made it my own. But one thing I do: forgetting what lies behind and straining forward to what lies ahead…" Philippians 3:13

Give your children something worth fighting for! As you think about conversations with your children about sex, you have an opportunity to paint a picture that will stir their hearts and motivate them to press on. Whatever image you choose, set before your children something that will encourage them to strain forward, towards something great.

> *"You shall love the LORD your God with all your heart and with all your soul and with all your might. And these words that I command you today shall be on your heart. You shall teach them diligently to your children, and shall talk of them when you sit in your house, and when you walk by the way, and when you lie down, and when you rise." Deuteronomy 6:5-7*

There is perfect, beautiful clarity in God's word. Teach your children diligently to love the Lord with all of their hearts, with all of their souls and with all of their might. Certainly this practice will overflow into every area of their lives.

As you begin to think about your message to your children about sex, I encourage you to base it on God's good and perfect word. Let what God says shape your words and thoughts. What do you want your children to understand about sex? The Bible holds deep truths that stem from our identity in Christ. It is a fitting place to begin the process of thinking about an overarching message about sexuality.

A simple reminder: give it time. Your message may not crystallize immediately. Give it time and continue the conversations to develop clarity. For the sake of our children, we want this to be a positive, godly message. This banner message will embody your overall plan of influence. Let's consider your first assignment and the ultimate goal of this first step: Can you summarize your vision and message in one sentence? It does not need to be more than that—consider one clear and concise sentence that articulates your message.

IN HIS IMAGE

We have talked through many helpful steps and things to consider when it comes to creating a message for our children to hear. It is helpful to remind ourselves of something deeply profound and simply stated: we were created in God's image. That should change our entire worldview. If we believe that to be true, what does that mean for our lives?

It means that God didn't make us to figure out life on our own. He made us to depend on Him, to reflect Him in every aspect of our lives. If we believe that we are made in God's image, that truth reminds us that our vision of sexuality must reflect God's very good design. Because of God's goodness, He changes us and breathes life into our message for our children.

What is the vision you want your children to have about sex? From there, your message—the words that you use—will reflect that vision, giving you a focus and a vocabulary that will clarify what you really want to communicate. Your message will give purpose to all of your conversations and also help redefine the choices you make in parenting.

Creating a message based on a specific vision is the most important of the five steps in this book. It will be a blessing to the way that you parent. This critical step allows you and your spouse to familiarize yourself with your core beliefs and principles. As Dave and I opened up conversations about our beliefs, our pasts and our principles, we developed our message: Sex is a gift from God for marriage. We wanted to emphasize the beauty and the boundaries that God had made clear to us. This simple sentence gave our conversations context and clarity. We could always go back to it as a point of reference.

Your message may be shorter, longer or even completely different. That's the beauty of individual families! It is most important that your message reflects what you believe God wants your children to understand about sex. The security of having a clear message makes every conversation purposeful. In the five-step process of learning to talk to your children, you will encounter many blessings. But at the beginning of this process, discussing our past while considering the future, all in light of God's word, will result in a clear message. We can hardly overestimate how that message will be a blessing to our children's future. Having a vision beforehand is essential.

What message are you creating for your children? Your words, actions and body language contribute as well. Little ears and eyes are always listening and watching. Children will learn the most about life from watching their parents. Being made in the image of God is the most important identity that you can teach your child. How does your message point your children to this identity?

WHAT IF I DON'T FIT THAT MOLD?

My hope is that, regardless of your parenting situation, you feel welcomed into this very important process. Since all families look different, everyone will be reading this book from a different perspective. Perhaps you and your spouse are not on the same page when it comes to creating a message and vision about sexuality. It is important to explore what the root of that difference may be. As you pray together and seek God's purpose for your child's future, I hope you can find a message that you both embrace.

Maybe you are a single parent and feel alone in this process. Though you may feel alone, the Lord will be with you. Remember that God's redemptive work is not contingent on our circumstances. He works in and through it all!

Divorced parenting situations look different from one situation to the next. Some divorced moms and dads are in a place to move through these steps together. Others are not. Even parents of adopted children find themselves in a unique situation. The important thing to remember is that as parents, we all share heartfelt concern for our children. That unites us all. And God's grace works in all situations. Together, we can commit to doing our part to protect our child's future health, happiness and sexual character.

Don't be disheartened if you don't fit a particular mold. God isn't surprised by your circumstances. He works in them, through them, and even in spite of them—for His glory and our good.

FOUNDATIONAL

We have covered a lot of ground so far! Your message offers a firm foundation and a great starting place. Where will you plant your feet as we continue on this journey? Your message should be simple and positive. For example: Sex is intended by God as a blessing. That is simple, and yet it communicates so much! How would you articulate that simple message to your children?

We have laid a firm foundation as we begin this process together. For the sake of simplicity, let's review step one:

Considering God's word, your experiences and your children's future, write a one-sentence message that will leave a godly vision on your children's sexual character.

As the pinnacle of God's creation, we were made in His image. I pray that that simple truth would encourage you to strive forward as you nurture your children towards a vision that will impact their future and most importantly, their understanding of who they are in Christ.

STEP TWO

**RESPECTFUL VOCABULARY ...
DEFINING MALE AND FEMALE ACCORDING TO GOD'S DESIGN**

"So God created man in his own image, in the image of God he created him; male and female he created them." Genesis 1:27

BUILDING ON THE FOUNDATION

We have made significant progress so far. Together as parents, we have laid a firm foundation. The work of creating a vision and overall message to share with your children is no small task. In fact, it is the most critical step we will take in this journey! Now that we are standing on a sure foundation, it is time to take a step forward: beginning the conversation.

The next step in this process is to consider your vocabulary. The words you choose to use matter! As our children grow in their understanding of the world, their vocabulary will expand to new horizons. The words that they hear at home will resonate deeply, and therefore, you have a great opportunity. How do you communicate with your children about their bodies? Which words do you use to distinguish between male and female? No doubt curious little minds will begin to wonder why boys are different from girls. Now is the time to start thinking about the words that you will use. Are they respectful words? Are they slang words borrowed from culture? Are they "cover-up words"? I came up with that phrase to describe the category of words that really don't give information. They simply "cover up" the real word. Sometimes they are funny little words (what I call wingy-wangy-words) that we make up to avoid something that seems awkward.

For instance, a "cover-up" example is the word "privates." Using the word "privates" is still a polite term in public, but it becomes a "cover-up word" if it is not expanded at home to include medical words. Many people use this word with the hope that it will encompass everything "personal" and "private" that really shouldn't be talked about anyway. The use of these types of words will limit future conversations. Each step in this journey is important. Let's grow together as we learn the weightiness of the words we use.

BEAUTY IN DESIGN

God was beautifully meticulous in His design. Let's take a look back at the beginning of Genesis to see His intention:

"So God created man in his own image, in the image of God he created him; male and female he created them." Genesis 1:27

From the beginning, God's design was full of great beauty. He crafted us—male and female—after His own image. Understanding your identity and your child's identity as image-bearers of the Lord Almighty will radically transform the way you think and live. He designed us all so that we would reflect His image. What a story! Beyond that, God created each of us with a specific gender. We see it here in the beginning of Genesis—God created male and female, both image-bearers, but distinctively and sexually unique. Sexuality was distinguished from the beginning of time. That is a glorious place to begin our conversation about words.

We can either diminish or honor the beauty of God's gift of sexuality with the words we use. So our words must really matter! Remember a thought from earlier in this book: the culture is yelling. What are your children hearing first? Are they learning about sexuality from their parents or from the new TV show? As parents, we have the privilege to speak first. As you probably notice, the current culture has created a perspective on sexuality that is far from the truth of God's word. Jokes, music and even slang have a way of dragging God's perfect creation through the mud. Many of the movies, TV shows and songs that fill our every day lives diminish what God said was *"fearfully and wonderfully made"* (Psalm 139:14).

It becomes our work as parents—and even as believers—to re-sensitize our ears. We must become aware of the words we have borrowed from a culture that does not acknowledge God's design. We often use these words without thinking, but the Lord intends to reshape our words after His. As we examine our words, we should ask ourselves: Are our words respectful and edifying? When we start to use words differently, there will be a ripple effect on how we teach our children. We share an opportunity as parents to teach our children about the beauty of their bodies. Our words and attitudes have the potential to point our children to that beauty or to belittle their bodies. Either way, we are shaping our children's understanding of who the Lord is and how He made them.

> **We must become aware of the words we have borrowed from a culture that does not acknowledge God's design.**

I invite you to begin the process of thinking about the vocabulary you will use to teach your children about their bodies and sexuality. How will those words shape their understanding? I recommend the use of medical terminology. The use of proper terms, as medically defined, will move their focus from cultural slang towards God's design.

THE TIME IS NOW!

There is something really sweet and calming about bath time. Sometimes. It is a time either to begin a new day or to prepare for bedtime. It is also an opportunity to begin simple conversations with your child. Bath time is the perfect time to introduce medical terminology. By pointing out elbows, a nose, toes and knees, your children will begin to learn and appreciate the proper name of different body parts. It is helpful to begin using proper names—of everything—in an appropriate manner in early childhood. Ankle and knuckle and earlobe and freckle sound just as funny to them as the words we are shying away from. The longer we wait to introduce the true, medical words, the more awkward it becomes later!

Now perhaps your babies are no longer babies and you are starting to feel like you missed the boat. Not at all! If you didn't start out early using medical terminology, it is not too late to start. You can introduce the terms by talking about babies and how they are uniquely boys or girls from the very beginning. Children are often curious about other babies, so take advantage of that opportunity! Whenever you begin to use these proper words, being intentional will set you up for future conversations.

Using correct terminology with your children while they are young is a great advantage. Two key things will begin to happen. First of all, you will become the authority on the subject. Your children are likely to come to you with any and all questions if they believe that you have answers. As they see your knowledge, you will begin to claim your rightful place as the loving authority in their lives. Additionally, using medical terminology will normalize the words you are using. Down the road, as conversations progress with your child, the terminology will not be a distraction from the actual information you want them to hear.

FEELING A LITTLE RELUCTANT?

I know what you are probably thinking, because I thought the same thing—if we tell our children the proper, medical words, they will have them in their vocabulary! They might be likely to share their new words with others (undoubtedly in front of your in-laws or loudly in the line at the grocery store). The reality is, you will probably experience a moment or two of laughter mixed with panic. So it is also important to seek opportunities to talk with your children about the appropriate times to talk about body parts. Help them to know that using the correct words at home is healthy and important. Invite them to ask questions and to use those words to better understand how God made them. But also give them an understanding of the importance of being polite and modest in public conversations. I hope you will find great joy in teaching your children appropriate boundaries that honor the Lord and their bodies.

LOOKING FOR THE RIGHT OPPORTUNITY

Apart from introducing the proper names of elbows, ears and knees in the bathtub, be on the lookout for an opportunity to introduce the medical terminology that distinguishes sexuality. We found a perfect opportunity when our neighbors brought home a new baby. Here is an idea of how that conversation unfolded:

Little boy: *"Mommy, will the baby be a boy or a girl?"*
Mom: *"Honey, I don't know yet. But as soon as the baby is born, the parents will know right away! Can you guess how they will know?*
Little boy: *"If it's a girl, she will have a bow, and if it's a boy he won't."*

Mom (I couldn't help but giggle at that response): *"As soon as a baby is born, the doctor will be able to tell. If it's a boy, he will have a penis, and if it's a girl, she will have a vagina. You don't get these special parts later in life, you are born that way! Babies are born either a boy or a girl. God decided what you would be before you were born."*

Talking about a new baby offered the perfect opportunity to present the medical terminology and also to talk about God's design of male and female. What beautiful truths to unfold before your children! As a side note, there is another benefit to children knowing medical terminology. They will be able to clearly identify the different parts if, Lord forbid, there should ever be any abuse or questionable activity. Children are empowered with the information of proper terminology, and it allows them to be very clear in communicating with you.

HEARING IT IN YOUR VOICE, SEEING IT IN YOUR LIFE

Let's take a moment and look at our role as parents. In thinking about our vocabulary with our children, it is also important to take note of our own actions and attitudes as well. Our children need to hear our voice and also watch our lives. Sometimes that is a very humbling reality of parenting!

Take a few moments for some honest self-evaluation. Is there anything you are watching or listening to or reading that could get in the way of what you are saying? Remember that little eyes and ears notice details! Many of us have heard the principle that "more is caught than taught." There is much truth to that. However, I believe that both teaching and catching will happen in families. Sometimes you will have the opportunity to share something "new" with your children. Other times, they will come to you with what they have heard at school or recess. It is crucial to remember that your child goes to school with classmates that have older brothers and sisters who likely share worlds of new information with their siblings. Your firstborn six-year-old is more than likely sitting next to a six-year-old who is the youngest of four. Her classmate brings new words and experiences to the classroom without even realizing it. I was always amazed by some of the topics of conversation that would pop up in carpool after school!

When I was a young mom, there was a daytime show that I enjoyed watching. I began to notice, however, that the show didn't line up with what I wanted to teach my children. For me as a parent, the best decision was to stop watching it. It is tough to parent these days! I had to make sacrifices (some were easier than others), but God graciously shows us what is best and what we can let go of. As I began to fight for conversations and growth with my children, fighting against the culture and even my own preferences became less overwhelming.

NOTICE THE PROGRESS!

Take a step back—notice the progress! In a small, but significant way, you have started the conversation with your children about sex! After prayer and conversation with your spouse or even on your own, you have taken the next step in "talking." That is a huge, first step!

You have given your children words that help me identify themselves and others as male and female, both made in God's image. You have pointed out how little boys and little girls were made with parts that are very good to God and important to His plan. As we talk about creation, we can teach our children to respect and not be ashamed of what God made in the garden. We can be clear and modest at the same time as we look to the Lord our Designer, who said it was all very good.

> **As we talk about creation, we can teach our children to respect and not be ashamed of what God made in the garden.**

ROOTED IN GOD'S WORD

Let's get back to the basics. For each and every step of this process, God's word is the foundation. He gives us clear guidance about sexuality and His very good creation, male and female.

"For you formed my inward parts; you knitted me together in my mother's womb. I praise you, for I am fearfully and wonderfully made. Wonderful are your works; my soul knows it very well." Psalm 139:13-14

Embrace the opportunity to teach your children about how they were made—fearfully and wonderfully. We were each crafted in God's image. He knows every cell in our bodies, for He knit them together. This is a huge perspective to give your children. God's handiwork is most spectacularly seen in us—His creation, male and female.

"See to it that no one takes you captive by philosophy and empty deceit, according to human tradition, according to the elemental spirits of the world, and not according to Christ. For in him the whole fullness of deity dwells bodily, and you have been filled in him, who is the head of all rule and authority." Colossians 2:8-10

Mentor your children towards Christ. Teach them how captivating it is to live for Him, to base their lives on Him. And through it all, pray for them! Pray that your children would find Christ to be abundantly fulfilling. Pray that they would live their lives in joyful submission to Christ.

> *"I will walk with integrity of heart within my house; I will not set before my eyes anything that is worthless." Psalm 101:2-3*

What a bold and beautiful goal! Think about what you set before your eyes. Think about what your children hear and see in your home. Are you creating a home environment that will challenge them to live with integrity of heart?

> *"Let your speech always be gracious, seasoned with salt, so that you may know how you ought to answer each person." Colossians 4:6*

Your speech matters! So much of what our children learn happens at home. Your prayerful consideration of how you teach them sexual terminology is well worth it!

God's word is a deep well of encouragement and guidance. Dig deep! He gives us all we need for teaching our children about His very good design.

THE PERFECT PLACE TO BEGIN

At the end of this chapter, we are arriving at a great place to begin future conversations. Determining the vocabulary that you want to use with your children will set you up for future conversations about sexuality. Don't shy away from using proper, medical terminology that will help your children honor their bodies and understand how God made them.

    Helping them to know the loving God who made them will affect every area of their lives in the years to come. What a blessing to begin the journey early! The conversations will continue, Lord willing. But for now, you are in the perfect place to take the next step.

STEP THREE

THE STORY OF BIRTH ...
EXPLAINING GOD'S MIRACLE OF BIRTH

"Be fruitful and multiply and fill the earth and subdue it…" Genesis 1:28

It is early on Saturday morning. The house is quiet and the subtle smell of coffee makes its way through the kitchen and to the table where you are reading the morning paper. Suddenly the faint pitter-patter of little feet is coming down the hall. Your young child quietly climbs into the chair next to you, ready for some breakfast and a new day. But this morning seems a little different from others. There is a look of thought and curiosity in his face today. Pausing to clear his little throat, he murmurs the question that is on his mind. *"Daddy, how will that baby get out of Mommy's tummy?"*

Your growing family is expecting another baby in a few short months and so there have been plenty of conversations revolving around what it will be like to have a baby brother or sister. But this question is requesting a little bit more detail. A great opportunity as arrived.

Smiling and nodding your head, you sit down and begin a simple conversation with your inquisitive toddler. *"I'm so glad you asked me that, buddy. Because I have news for you: the baby isn't in Mommy's tummy. The baby is in Mommy's uterus. Sometimes the uterus is called a 'womb' and it is a special place designed by God where the baby can grow. Everything the baby needs is inside the womb. After about 40 weeks, the baby is ready to live outside of the uterus. When that time comes, we call it birth. And that is when you will finally get to meet your baby brother or sister!"*

With a wrinkled brow, he points out an observation. *"Why does it look like the baby is in Mommy's tummy?"* You chuckle because he has a great point! *"Well that's because the uterus is close to Mommy's tummy. But the tummy is for food, just like my tummy and your tummy. That would be a messy place for a baby to grow! So God made a different place that only women have, so that they can carry the baby inside of them."*

That seemed to clear up a few of his questions, but in between spoonfuls of cereal he comes up with another thought. *"Hmm. Well, then how does the baby get out of the uterus?"* This is such a sweet moment, you realize. It is such an opportunity to show your child the miraculous work of God. *"By God's design, a baby is ready to be born after living for about 40 weeks in Mommy's uterus. The muscles around the uterus begin to push the baby out—and the mommy can feel this! She knows that this is the beginning of birth, so she usually goes to the hospital or calls for a midwife to come and help her. When the muscles get really tight, this is called a contraction."*

His little eyes are fixed on you as if he is hearing the most fascinating story he's ever heard. So you continue, *"The baby is pushed by those contractions out of the uterus, through the birth canal and out of a special opening called the vagina that is between the mother's legs. When the baby comes out of the mother, it is still connected to her by the umbilical cord. So the doctor will snip that cord and now the baby has arrived! A brand new person is born."*

Now sitting on his knees and leaning over the table he exclaims in excitement, *"Wow! I can't wait to meet my little brother or sister!"* It is important to give him all of the facts, so you tag on one more thought, *"Now sometimes when a baby is leaving the uterus, the baby wiggles so that he or she can't fit through the birth canal. The doctor knows just what do to. He is able to make an opening with his instruments close to where the baby is and lift the baby out. This is called a Caesarean section. That's a big, long word, so sometimes people just call it a C-section. That is how your cousin Ella was born."* You smile and add, *"That's why her head is so pretty!"*

BE FRUITFUL AND MULTIPLY

Even as early as Genesis, God's word is clear in commanding how we are to live and flourish as His creation. After His creation of Adam and Eve, the Lord was forthright in giving them specific directions: *"Be fruitful and multiply"* (Genesis 1:28). God envisioned the earth filled with His creation—including humans, made in His image. And He gave this very special task of filling creation to husbands and wives. In the union of marriage, a husband and wife become one flesh for the purpose of companionship and bearing fruit.

As your children grow up, their curiosity will grow as well. Whether it is with a new brother or sister, or even a neighbor, sooner or later they will want to know about babies and how they get out of a mommy's "tummy." The birth of new creation—humans and even flowers and animals—is a natural part of life. Children are very perceptive when it comes to noticing the order and progression of life. So as those little questions begin to come your way, it is good to be prepared to answer in a manner that will continue to paint the picture of God's beautiful design. And it doesn't have to happen in just one conversation. Consider the multiple, simple conversations that you can have with your child to help them understand the miracle of birth.

> **So as those little questions begin to come your way, it is good to be prepared to answer in a manner that will continue to paint the picture of God's beautiful design.**

Similar to the conversation at the beginning of this chapter, you have the opportunity to share with your child in a way that will teach them and point them to the Lord. When do these little, teachable moments happen at your house?

Maybe it is in the early hours of the morning over a bowl of cereal. Or perhaps it is in between story time and prayers at bedtime. Enjoy these moments and make them count towards your children growing in awe of their Creator. Speak with awe in your voice as you talk about birth—be amazed with your children!

THE JOY OF STORYTELLING

One of my favorite parts of being a mom was telling and reading stories to my children. We would read classics and create far away worlds in our imaginations. Storytelling is a beautiful way of painting a picture with words. So as we continue on this journey together, let's make time for stories. Telling your children the story of birth will be one of the fun parts of this process! It should be a joy to teach your children about how God designed our bodies to be fruitful and multiply.

Have you ever talked to your child about a newborn baby? Children are mesmerized to hear the stories of how babies are born. This goes for puppies, kitties and of course, humans. The story of a new birth is captivating to kids' imagination, especially when it is about a new baby girl or boy. Chances are, they will once again be dazzled with new terminology like uterus, birth canal and umbilical cord. Remember our thoughts on using medical vocabulary—this is another chance to help them understand the way God made us.

A special place to start is by telling your children about the day they were born. They will most certainly be intrigued when they realize that the story is about them! Sharing details about that special day will paint the picture and help them stand in wonder of how God made them. Birthdays come around every year—what a beautiful and natural opportunity to share that story year after year! Details will show children how very special they are in God's sight and in your family.

Prepare yourself to share this story over and over again. You will become a champ at reliving the birthdays of your children. They will love to hear it and probably ask for an encore time and time again. No doubt, your world was forever changed with the birth of your children. Help them to grasp how special and beautiful that day was for your family. As they come to understand how they were born, it will be natural to look at the world around them and wonder about other children, babies and birthdays.

CART BEFORE THE HORSE?

You might be thinking that we missed a very important step to this process. As parents, we know that conception comes before birth. So perhaps you are wondering: *are we putting the cart before the horse by telling our children about birth? Don't we have to cover conception first?* Not necessarily. Of course conception is a big part of the equation and we will get to that point. However, it is important to take note of where your children are. They are usually first curious about birth… and then conception. I have found it to be helpful to follow their developmental curiosity instead of the biological order of things.

We know that there is a lot that happens before a baby is born, but children typically start with the newborn baby and then move backwards in their understanding. Questions about birth begin to pop up as early as the age of 3, or occasionally sooner. Sometimes the birth of younger siblings or cousins will spur on the questions. It helps to be ready for this step, as it will be very natural for children to be curious. It is amazing to notice how children are natural problem solvers. When children see a pregnant mother, they want to figure out how that baby will get out of there. It is perplexing for them!

So their first question is not usually, *"How did that baby get in there?"* But don't worry, that will come soon enough. They are first concerned about an exit strategy and the wellbeing of the baby inside. *"How will he or she get out?"* As each step unfolds, I hope that you will welcome the opportunity to tell them about God's beautiful design. Take one step at a time. By God's grace we will get to where we are going.

A HEARTFELT NOTE TO ADOPTIVE PARENTS

Adoptive mothers and fathers fulfill a unique role and have an amazing calling in the lives of their children. I pray that if your story is one of adoption, you will see how beautifully your story is in God's grand design. He puts families together for His good purposes. Adoption involves multiple stories that have been sewn together: the story of the child, the birth mother and the story of the parents. Together, these stories create a beautiful tapestry of a new family.

I would like to take a moment to speak heart to heart with parents who are blessed with an adopted son or daughter. God's story in your family is an incredible picture of the gospel. As believers, we have all been adopted as children of the Living God. Through Jesus, we have the right to be heirs with Christ because of what He did on our behalf. Truly, as Christians we all share the story of adoption because we have received the inheritance as members of God's family. When I consider families who grow through the blessing of adoption, I think about the beautiful picture that is unfolding. As an adoptive parent, you are modeling the gospel truth of God's love for your children.

Adoption could be part of your family's story for many different reasons. Perhaps your story involves infertility. Or maybe the Lord has placed the deep desire for adoption on your heart. Whatever your story is, adopted children will need a few more questions answered than biological children. They will still need to hear your clear message and the basic biology of birth and conception. But just like all children, they are filled with curious wonder. Adopted children are usually curious about birth from the beginning, because they hear about a "birth mother." If you are prepared, what a beautiful opportunity!

It is important to have early conversations about birth with your adopted child, or at least be ready for them. And it is helpful to keep four things in mind: your specific message (the one sentence assignment from step one), the basic biology (steps two through five), your child's unique story, and your own unique story. With this in mind, it is good to choose your words carefully so that at the end of the day, our adopted children grow up knowing the deep love that covers them. Remind them of the love of their birth mother, who wanted what was best for them. And of course, highlight your love for them—their "forever parents" who will guide them under God's direction and grace. Ultimately, pray that they would see that their heavenly Father's adopting love is the greatest blessing of all.

Adopted children are often curious about why adoption is necessary. So how can we explain the different reasons to them? By God's grace, children who are adopted come from different circumstances and stories. Invite them to see the different reasons and God's sovereignty through it all.

Sometimes a pregnant woman cannot raise her child due to finances or circumstances. She seeks help from a family who can lovingly raise her child.

Sometimes it is impossible for a husband and wife to have a baby. Perhaps there is an issue with the sperm or the eggs. Whatever the reason, the wife is unable to conceive, give birth or carry a child.

> **It is beautiful to remember that God values adoption so much that He describes us, His beloved children, as adopted.**

Sometimes a couple shares a deep desire to adopt a child, even though God has blessed them with biological children. Maybe they have met a child in need of adoption and know in their hearts that he or she is meant for their family. Other times adoption happens internationally—the beautiful blend of families and cultures.

Whatever the reason, adoption is precious to God and close to His heart. Though the picture of the gospel in adoption is beautiful to behold, I also understand that it may be painful for the adoptive mother to tell the story of birth because she hasn't experienced that particular birth herself. It is beautiful to remember that God values adoption so much that He describes us, His beloved children, as adopted. Though we were not born into God's family, we are called into His family by the Holy Spirit. Every child—biological and adopted—matters deeply to God. I hope that you and your children grow in a deep understanding of the Lord's particular and overwhelming love in your life.

NEW LIFE

For all of us, God's plan is magnificent. The story of birth is a beautiful picture of His design and plan. The Lord weaves families together for His glory through childbirth and through the gift of adoption. So whether you are a parent to biological children or adopted children or both, you have the privilege of talking with them about that design.

The story of birth will teach children about how God fills the earth that He created. It will also help them to understand how special they are to your family. Mom and Dad, you have the joy of showing your children that they were made in God's image and born to live a life that is special and set apart for God's glory. What a delight! A new life is something to celebrate. The story of a new life—beginning at birth—is one that you can retell to your children, over and over again. God gets the glory every time.

STEP FOUR

GOD'S DESIGN OF REPRODUCTION …
EXPLORING GOD'S DESIGN IN ALL OF CREATION

"Behold, I have given you every plant yielding seed that is on the face of the earth, every tree with seed in its fruit." Genesis 1:29

Let's go back to the beach. Do you remember that beautiful day we imagined at the beginning of this book? From your sandy beach chair, you watch your children near the water's edge. They are still running and playing in the surf. Their attention jumps from creature to creature—a world of living, breathing things all around them! Birds fly overhead and swoop down towards the beach for a closer look. The ocean is teeming with life—fish jumping and tiny creatures scurrying.

As your children trace the ocean's tide along the sand, they hurry up the beach, away from the water. They suddenly crouch down onto their knees and sit in an unusually quiet wonder. Intrigued by their sudden silence, you make your way towards their sandy perch. Something extraordinary is happening. Just a few feet away, you notice the focus of their attention: a sea turtle nest, hatching before your eyes. Joining your children in the sand, you sit quietly as the ground begins to shuffle. Baby turtles hatch and make their way to the surface of the beach. One after another, they break out of their soft shells and scamper toward the daylight above their sandy nest.

Your children sit still and silent, captivated by God's beauty unfolding. Suddenly the nest, once covered in a mound of sand, is moving in a frenzied state. The baby turtles are making their way towards the water. Now growing into a little army, they dash into the surf and disappear into the waves. As the last three turtles emerge and make towards the sea, your children slowly stand and quietly follow the scuttle. One by one the last three disappear into the waves. The miracle of new life has just unfolded before the watchful eyes of your children.

It is incredible to see the miracle of God's living things in His creation. Sharing nature with your children provides the perfect classroom for taking the next step in this journey as parents. A day at the beach or an afternoon in the backyard will help your children grow in their sense of wonder at God's design.

ALL LIVING THINGS

Now that you have shared the story of birth with your children, it is time to take the next step: understanding God's design of reproduction in all living things. Together, we have taken a natural progression of things in our conversations. Children are most curious about birth and then conception. Similarly, before talking about conception, it is helpful to introduce the natural reproduction of all things that God made, particularly with an interest in seeds and eggs.

The most natural progression, of course, comes from God's word. In Genesis, God told Adam and Even to "be fruitful and multiply." Then He said,

"And God said, 'Behold, I have given you every plant yielding seed that is on the face of all the earth, and every tree with seed in its fruit. You shall have them for food. And to every beast of the earth and to every bird of the heavens and to everything that creeps on the earth, everything that has the breath of life, I have given every green plant for food.' And it was so. And God saw everything that he had made, and behold, it was very good. And there was evening and there was morning, the sixth day."
Genesis 1:29-31

Once again, the Bible offers the perfect outline for our conversations. I pray that His word will continue to be our guiding light as we parent in all areas, especially in these conversations about sexuality. God's word is very clear in explaining how living things are made. Pointing your children to His word—and to His creation—is the perfect way to start this next conversation. From the beginning, He has surrounded us with seasonal examples of His sweet design.

INTENTIONALITY

The world is your classroom. Everything you need to teach your children about the Lord and His design can be seen in His creation. You can use nature as your textbook in observing the wonder of reproduction. Just step outside!

Children are captivated by all creeping and crawling things… whether it makes you squirm or not. They love to dig and find and ask questions. Whether it is watching a bird's nest through the kitchen window or watching sea turtles hatch and race towards the sea, children are already fixated on the world around them. Simply take advantage of the opportunities! Take a look at your normal, day-to-day routine. Find moments that are already part of your week with your children. Most of the time, the perfect opportunity is right in front of you—you just have to be intentional about turning it into something more than a fleeting moment.

> **The world is your classroom. Everything you need to teach your children about the Lord and His design can be seen in His creation. You can use nature as your textbook in observing the wonder of reproduction. Just step outside!**

Consider the mundane routine of snack time. What a perfect opportunity to turn a snack into a learning time. Give this a try. The next time you slice open an apple for snack, wait to throw away the core. Instead, sit down with your child and show them the seed inside. Point out how deeply the seed is nestled safely inside the core. As they hold the tiny seeds in their hands, talk about how the seeds, when planted and cared for, are responsible for another apple tree and another apple.

Explain how things work using the items in your kitchen. Inside every living thing is a piece (a seed) of what it takes to make the next living thing—"fruit" just like it! An apple seed will always make another apple. An orange seed will always make another orange. And a mama bird will always make a baby bird. God's creation is made to reproduce, again and again. That's how this beautiful world flourishes year after year!

Think about the opportunity of Halloween. While carving pumpkins together in October, wait before you throw out the gooey insides. Spread them out on a newspaper and look at the seeds together. Perhaps you can even try planting a few seeds in the backyard. I have found that giving children something to care for—like a plant in their room or in the backyard—is a simple way of showing them how God's world reproduces with proper care.

As you talk about seeds, observe with your child how they are tucked deep inside for their protection. Seeds must be cared for and protected for another living thing to exist one day. Do you see the connection to human reproduction? Helping your children see it in the world around them is the perfect place to begin.

BRINGING IT INTO THEIR WORLD

Sometimes the most teachable moments are the ones that are not created—they already exist. Moving into your child's world allows them to see things on their own level. Capture these moments! You can turn learning time into fun games. Think about the many different times during the day that involve food. Look towards lunch, snack time or even dinner, and challenge your child to play along. See if they can fine the seed in a strawberry, banana or cucumber. As they locate the different seeds, help them to become students of where those seeds live and how they are protected and cared for. Meals and snack times for young children can become important stepping-stones to learning and understanding.

Children are fascinated by what is going on around them. Take advantage of the spring. Step outside and be on the lookout for birds nesting around your home. Or maybe even a butterfly in its cocoon! As you watch life bud, bloom and grow around you, teach kids about how life happens through eggs. These tiny eggs are laid and protected and designed for new life.

I once knew a family who would happen upon a robin's nest every spring. Some years they would even find a baby robin, fallen from the nest! The family would devote time to watching the birds flourish in their back yard. What are some creative ways to watch new life unfold around you? Some families, depending on their circumstances and where they live, could even take on the family responsibility of incubating eggs and watching the whole process unfold. Obviously, every family is different and this isn't possible for some. But real life experience is certainly a blessing, if possible.

As you watch the world around you, paint a picture for your children that will invite them to be captivated by the miracle of God's design for brand new life. You don't have to have a chicken coop in your backyard (although, how wonderful if you do!) to learn these lessons together. Use what you have in your kitchen or find in your garden or even at the grocery store. The evidence is all around you—the world is your perfect classroom for pointing your family to God's design.

> **As you watch the world around you, paint a picture for your children that will invite them to be captivated by the miracle of God's design for brand new life.**

The Lord started something remarkable in the Garden of Eden. And it continues today, though it is certainly different in a fallen world. My attempt at a garden is evidence of that truth. But His design is still there for us to see and wonder about with our children. From pumpkin carving to summer picnics with watermelons, to growing squash in the backyard, God has given us wholesome pictures of His bounty and creativity. As parents, we have the high privilege of pouring into our children and shaping their understanding of God's world and creation. Let's take advantage of what is right before us!

THE PERFECT SPRINGBOARD

Imagine that you are watching a mother jaybird build her nest outside of your kitchen window. As you watch the process unfold with your children, you are finding yourself in the perfect spot of opportunity. Observing and discussing reproduction in creation is a natural part of raising children. Having little conversations about how life begins in plants and seeds is a subtle way to lay the foundation for what is to come in future conversations.

As you talk about seeds and eggs and God's creative order, you will be equipped for that amazing question, *"Mommy, how did that baby get in there?"* Perhaps that question still makes your stomach turn. But hopefully, you are finding confidence with each little step we take together. That question will inevitably come—but have the assurance that the small conversations that you started a while back will set you up to be ready. So take a deep breath—we are laying the foundation and moving forward one small but significant step at a time.

Let's celebrate where we are and think about where we have been so far in this book. At the beginning, we considered our overall message and the image we want to set for our children's sexuality. From there, we talked about using proper vocabulary that will help them understand the unique ways that God made male and female. Next, we discussed fun and unique ways to talk about the story of birth and how the beginning of a new life is wonderful and intriguing to young minds. Now we find ourselves discussing the design of reproduction. Each step builds on the one before, but stacked up together, we have covered some serious ground.

We have had a series of small conversations. And so far, nothing has been too difficult. I hope you feel the same way. Step by step, you have been building trust and sharing information that will lead to the next little visit: one about conception. Hopefully, you have found each step to be natural and simple. Realize that these simple steps hold tremendous value. Though they may seem like insignificant baby steps, they are invaluable to your growth as a family and to your children's understanding of God's design. You are beginning the very purposeful journey of shaping your child's sexual character by providing information and pointing them to God all in the same step-by-step process.

SWIMMING UPSTREAM

Through this process I want to invite you to something different—something that our American culture might find strange. As parents, I want you to see the beauty of abandoning the American tradition of the fear-based, one-time-only "TALK" when your child reaches age 12. Cramming everything about God's design and sexuality into ONE uncomfortable conversation is an overwhelming thought, no doubt. Instead, I hope that you see this beautiful alternative.

> **In beginning these simple conversations when your children are young, you will be using God's more effective plan of teaching your children as you do life together.**

In beginning these simple conversations when your children are young, you will be using God's more effective plan of teaching your children as you do life together. A vision for this kind of life together is rooted in God's word:

"You shall love the LORD your God with all your heart and with all your soul and with all your might. And these words that I command you today shall be on your heart. You shall teach them diligently to your children, and shall talk of them when you sit in your house, and when you walk by the way, and when you lie down, and when you rise." Deuteronomy 6:5-7

God has described his way of passing on the faith from one generation to another. The Lord commands parents and gives them the privilege to saturate the soil of the next generation with His word. What a beautiful vision and powerful motivation.

TRUTH OF GOD'S WORD

As you stop to observe God's beauty and design, look to God's word as you pray and think about this important step in talking with your children. Here are some passages that I have found to be instrumental in preparing my thoughts:

"In the beginning, God created the heavens and the earth." Genesis 1:1

Stir your children's imagination with thoughts of God being the Creator of all things—from blades of grass to flying sparrows to human beings. They can learn at a young age that the Lord is the creative and masterful Creator of everything that they see. What a perfect place to begin!

"And God said, 'Let the earth sprout vegetation, plants yielding seed, and fruit trees bearing fruit in which is their seed, each according to its kind, on the earth.' And it was so. The earth brought forth vegetation, plants yielding seed according to their own kinds, and trees bearing fruit in which is their seed, each according to its kind. And God saw that it was good." Genesis 1:11-12

In the beginning of creation, the Bible talks about seeds and fruit—the very topic we are talking about in this step. The Lord built a pattern and rhythm into His creation. All living things grow from small seed. The beginning of something extraordinary comes from tiny, hidden seeds.

> *"For what can be known about God is plain to them, because God has shown it to them. For his invisible attributes, namely, his eternal power and divine nature, have been clearly perceived, ever since the creation of the world, in the things that have been made. So they are without excuse." Romans 1:19-20*

Creation points to God's majesty and supremacy. As you point your children to God's creation, they will see His design. According to His goodness, He planned it that way! God's glorious creation speaks for itself. It will be such a blessing to your family if you let the Lord's design and creation do the talking. So step outside. Enjoy a bright and beautiful classroom with your children as you live life together.

STEP FIVE

THE STORY OF CONCEPTION ...
REVEALING THE ONENESS AND FRUITFULNESS OF GOD'S DESIGN FOR MARRIAGE

"Therefore a man shall leave his father and his mother and hold fast to his wife, and they shall become one flesh." Genesis 2:24

Together, we are approaching the culmination of laying the foundational information and values for talking to our children about sex. For years to come, you will see that it all started with these five simple steps. The deep and basic foundations for a lifetime of conversations have been laid. We have been laying a foundation for conversations with our children that will be a blessing. Take a look at where we have been. Each step along this journey has been significant. Perhaps you initially thought that "talking to your children about sex" only involved this final step. However, we have taken a different approach. We have built towards this conversation, so that it is in the context of all of the other conversations.

We have moved away from the "one time only" sex talk and moved towards a series of smaller conversations that highlight God's good design. And we have chosen a path that gives our children a unique perspective—one that focuses on the creative design of our Maker and His intentional plan for those who have been made in His image. Learning to talk to your children about sex is about so much more than what we see on the surface. It can be about instilling in them a sense of wonder at God's goodness and His particular plan for their lives and sexuality.

Before we take this big step forward, it is important to reflect on the significance of each prior step. I hope that you see each one as simple—and yet profound. After many small conversations, you can now find yourself in a position to take the next step—talking about conception. Considering all of the ground we have covered, this last conversation doesn't seem so daunting anymore. There is something empowering about standing in this place, knowing all that we have talked about together.

THE QUESTION

Imagine that you are sitting across the table from your child. You are both enjoying a bowl of ice cream for dessert. With a chocolate-rimmed smirk, your little one asks a question with curiosity and perplexity. *"So Mommy, how did that baby get in there?"*

Chances are, up to this point, your child has been content with the new understanding of how a baby is born. That is why we covered birth before conception. But as your children's curiosity and understanding grow, they want to know more. I know that it seems like a big step, but it is a good and natural progression when your child finally wants to understand more about how all of this works.

Children are really not asking to know about sex, they are asking to know how things happen and the answer is sex. We get to give the surprising answer in a way that is not disturbing, but rather enlightening and age appropriate. Once again, we give them answers that point to God and point to a pattern of parenting that says, *"There is more to come, but I have given you great information for now."*

Before anything else—take time to rejoice! I want you to realize the magnitude of this moment. Your child is coming to YOU with their curious questions. Think of all the other places they could have turned to—friends, television, the internet or movies. And yet, they are looking to you. This is an exciting opportunity. I hope that you feel the victory of the moment. Before asking anyone else or even hearing about it at school, your child is looking to you, the loving authority in his or her life, to learn about sex.

You have the opportunity to give them a God-centered perspective on sex. The TV shows and precocious classmates with older siblings have lost the battle. It is your privilege as the parent. This moment really is sweet.

When you hear that question or find an opportunity to talk about conception, realize that it is a holy time to point your child straight to God's word. We have been looking at Genesis 1 as our main reference for these conversations. For each step, we have followed the progression seen at the beginning of time. After God created everything, and male and female were fashioned in His image, Adam and Eve felt no shame in the Lord's good and perfect design. Marriage was blissful and pure. In Genesis 2, we read about how God made man and then fashioned woman to be a fitting helper for him. We also see a very important detail at the end of chapter 2:

> *"Therefore a man shall leave his father and his mother and hold fast to his wife, and they shall become one flesh. And the man and his wife were both naked and were not ashamed."* Genesis 2:24-25

Through the beautiful boundaries provided by God in marriage, Adam and Eve felt no shame because their relationship fit within God's good plan. The Bible is very clear about sexuality. No wonder it is the perfect resource for all of our parenting in this important area. Genesis 2 paints a picture of sexuality that later leads to conception in chapter 4 when Eve gives birth to Cain and Abel. As we prepare to answer that curious little question of *"how did that baby get in there,"* we can lean on God's Word for guidance.

FEARFULLY AND WONDERFULLY

There is always great fun to be had at the zoo. Perhaps going to the zoo is one of your family's favorite outings. Or maybe you have yet to experience the joy of taking your children to see lions and tigers and bears—in a safe and secure setting. Imagine for a moment that you are visiting the local zoo with your child. It is a beautiful spring day. The weather is ideal to bounce from exhibit to exhibit. You slowly make your way through the tanks of fish and through the canopy of trees, where playful monkeys are swinging. The next stop is the tiger cages.

Your little one clutches onto your hand as if it were a safety net as she walks towards the sprawling creature, enjoying a sunny spot on the other side of the glass. Not quite the neighborhood kitty! It is amazing to stand before something that you know is so powerful. And yet, you can stand in awe of the tigers with great assurance. You behold the incredible beauty and strength of the tigers with confidence because they are contained. Even a roar is muffled and wildly entertaining from behind glass!

Tigers elicit fear because they are powerful and majestic animals. You know enough to know that they are creatures capable of hunting, running and even killing. And yet they are unbelievably beautiful to enjoy from behind a secure boundary. Fear and wonder sit side by side—what a fascinating paradox! Beauty dances with terror.

One of my favorite passages in scripture is found in Psalm 139 and it perfectly fits with where we are on this journey:

"For you formed my inward parts; you knitted me together in my mother's womb. I praise you, for I am fearfully and wonderfully made. Wonderful are your works; my soul knows it very well. My frame was not hidden from you, when I was being made in secret, intricately woven in the depths of the earth. Your eyes saw my unformed substance; in your book were written, every one of them, the days that were formed for me, when as yet there was none of them." Psalm 139:13-16

To begin the conversation about conception, a good place to start is by looking at this passage and talking about those two simple words: fearfully and wonderfully. God's work to "knit" a baby together in a mother's womb is fearful and wonderful. I hope that you have enjoyed the opportunities to talk to your child about the intricacy of God's design in all things—from apples to baby birds to people. The way a baby is made—beginning as a tiny seed, buried deep inside a mother's womb—is awesome to consider.

Similarly, the act of making a baby—sex between a man and woman—is also fearful and wonderful. Begin your conversation by explaining that these two words sit side by side in God's word for a great reason.

PUTTING IT INTO WORDS

With the concept of "fearful and wonderful" in mind, it's now time to put our thoughts into words. Remember that the story you are telling your children does not need to be sensual. It needs to point clearly to God's design. This is also not a "lecture" conversation. So feel free to keep your thoughts and words simple, introducing "key players" such as God, husband, wife, seed, egg and new baby.

Craft a sentence or two based on your message and basic biology. My husband Dave and I crafted our conception conversation based on our message of *"Sex is a gift from God for marriage."* That was our starting point. I encourage you to think of the "conception conversations" in parts. When your young child is initially interested in learning more about how babies get started, all you need to offer is a first impression. Here's an example that might be helpful:

Young Child: *"How did that baby get in there?"*

Mother or Father: *"Well, I am so glad that you asked. You know what? By God's design, a husband and wife were made to fit together in a very special way. And when that happens, part of what is deep inside Daddy, the sperm, meets with part of what is deep inside Mommy, the egg, and that is what God uses to make the baby."*

It is really that simple. You are offering simple, basic, age appropriate information that will give them a first impression. Sometimes that answer satisfies their questions for a while. Realize that it won't be your last conversation, so you don't want or need to cover everything at once. The simple goal at this point is to pick them up and point their little feet in the direction you want them to go—towards your message. The vocabulary you choose to use in answering this question comes directly from your message in step one.

Think of sex as a symphony. At this point, you are simply giving them the introductory melody. If you think of sex as a masterpiece of art, you are giving them the charcoal sketch, pointing out the basic idea. As time goes on, you will complete the picture with more of the details. Also keep in mind that for each person, there is an important element of mystery for him or her to later discover in his or her own marriage.

As children grow in maturity, their questions will mature as well. They are curious to have a little bit more information. This is the opportunity to take the next step and share a few more details. Here is what I mean:

Young child: *"What do you mean 'fits together in a very special way'? What does that mean?"*

Mother or Father: *"Honey, it is pretty amazing how God designed for this to happen. Do you remember when I said that there is a part that is deep inside of Daddy? Well, that is called the sperm, or the seed like we have talked about before. The sperm needs to meet with the egg that is deep inside of Mommy for the baby to begin to grow. So this is how it happens: the husband places his penis inside of the wife's vagina. The sperm that is deep inside of the daddy travels through the penis and meets with the egg that is deep inside of the mommy. That is how a mommy and a daddy fit together and how the baby begins. God designed marriage for oneness and also for making babies."*

I hope that it helps to hear a few words that you can borrow and adjust for your own conversations. Sometimes it helps to hear it played out. As you share these details, you are sticking with basic biology (the mechanics) and God's design. So this is not disturbing information for children to hear. Isn't that surprising? However, these early conversations do not include information about pleasures or dangers. We are just sticking to the facts and pointing them to the Lord's plan.

Do you remember those funny and slightly embarrassing comments that toddlers love to make in the grocery line? This is another opportunity to teach them about the appropriateness of sharing information. Let your child know how pleased you are that YOU are the one to tell them this special information. These are details that parents want to share with their own children. Explain that it would not be appropriate for them to share this information with their friends, because all mommies and daddies get to decide when to share with their children. Hopefully, this will empower your child to realize that the information they now carry is special enough to handle with care.

> **Sometimes parents need to take the first step! If this is the case in your family, consider introducing the subject yourself by asking them a simple question: "Have you ever wondered?"**

Maybe your child is talkative and curious and these sample conversations perfectly fit your situation. I am so glad. But perhaps you have a precious child who never asks the questions that initiate conversations. That is perfectly normal. Sometimes parents need to take the first step! If this is the case in your family, consider introducing the subject yourself by asking them a simple question: *"Have you ever wondered?"* Have you ever wondered about…how a baby is born? How a baby is made? How girls and boys are made differently? How God designed living things to make new living things?

You might suggest to them that you were curious about those things when you were their age, but didn't know the right questions to ask. Initiating these conversations is sometimes the most loving thing to do. Some children have a sense of propriety and they don't want to put their parents in an uncomfortable position, so they never ask. I would encourage you not to leave them there, but to reach out in a way that gives them permission to be curious in a healthy way. Invite them to look to you, their parent, for accurate information. Guide them towards God's design. Show your willingness to engage them with this subject.

Your opportunity to talk about conception might look just like one of these situations and it might look totally different. Either way, be confident in the baby steps that we have all taken to get to this point. The Lord will guide our steps, even when our paths seem really different.

THINGS TO REMEMBER

The first step of this whole process is essential—remember back to when we talked about your message. As you begin this particular conversation about conception, keep your initial message and overall vision in the back of your mind. Before your child was even old enough to understand, what was your hope for their understanding about sexuality? Remind yourself of the image you hope your child will have of sex after this conversation about conception. Are you moving towards that message and goal?

As you talk about conception, also keep this in mind: talks of the pleasures and dangers of sex are best suited when your child is old enough—and mature enough—to understand what you are saying. Sometimes these conversations happen on down the road. So this first time that you talk about conception and how babies are made, it is not necessary to cover all of those details. A time will come when those conversations fit your child's maturity level.

Also remember that God's grace covers all our shortcomings and regretful memories. Maybe talking about conception with your child brings up things from your past that you regret. God's grace is at work in your child—but also in your life. We must embrace the gospel ourselves before we can pass it on to our children. God's grace wipes away all mistakes and areas of painful regret. Because of what Jesus has done, all things are new and clean for those who trust Him. Remember that your own slate has been wiped clean. As you recall His overwhelming grace in your own life, you can have great hope for your children and their generation. Dwell on God's goodness and faithfulness to you and then proceed with confidence.

BOUNDARIES FOR A REASON

Boundaries exist for a reason. As cows graze in a pasture, they enjoy safety because a fence marks a boundary that separates the pasture from the road. Those lines are drawn and kept for a reason. God has created boundaries for us because He understands the dangers of living without them. Help your child see the beauty of God-given boundaries.

Remember the tigers behind glass? They are stunning creatures to watch from behind safe boundaries. Think about the ocean. There is nothing more exhilarating than standing at the water's edge, watching the powerful waves roll in and feeling the mist splash your feet and face. The ocean is glorious because it is contained. When the waters rage outside of those defined boundaries—think of hurricanes or tsunamis—the ocean causes horrific disaster.

What about a fire? We are fascinated by its glow and warmth. And yet when fire leaves the safe boundaries of a candle or fireplace, it can cause devastation and hurt. Boundaries are necessary, and they are blessings from the Lord. In His goodness, God gave us boundaries for enjoying sex. He did this because He knew that sex has two very powerful components: fear and wonder. Talk to your children about these two aspects.

Sex is wonderful. It is designed by God, for the sanctity of marriage, to populate His created world with people who are made in His own image. God intended sex for GOOD. But there is another side to it.

Sex is fearful. Sadly, sex is widely and tragically abused by our culture. I pray that this book and the steps we are taking together will help us combat the perversion of God's very good design that we see all around us. Think of how different our world would be if our children understood the incredible magnitude of sex and the potential dangers of trying to enjoy it without its intended boundaries.

It is beautiful to realize that the boundaries of marriage actually offer freedom. Give your children an understanding of good, healthy boundaries in all areas of their lives, including sexuality.

GOD'S DESIGN

It is really quite simple. We enjoy the goodness of God's design when we understand our sexuality according to His plan. He designed human reproduction to happen through sex. The conception of a baby is a holy and mysterious thing. As you continue to paint a picture of God's design for your children, their questions will be more natural for you to answer.

Think about the impact that these early conversations can have on your child's future relationships and marriage! Do you ever dream about what your child will be like as an adult, as a husband or a wife? Dream for your children before they are old enough to dream for themselves. Pray that the Lord would give you a thriving marriage and a healthy vision of sexuality. That kind of relationship will obviously be a great blessing to you but also to your children as they watch you closely. As you dream, your actions will follow and conversations will naturally unfold.

Don't convince yourself that your kids are "too young" to talk about conception. Talk about boundaries, talk about the fearful and wonderful ways that babies are made. Also realize that you won't cover everything at once. You will hopefully have numerous opportunities for further conversations with your growing children. But by God's grace, the foundation has been laid, and the talking has begun.

PARTING THOUGHTS

As you secure the treasure of these conversations, you may have a sense of completion as you look at your child. They have been introduced to God's design for sex, and yet it is only the beginning. My hope and prayer through out this book is that you will leave feeling equipped and encouraged. I want you to be equipped to teach your children the beauty of God's wondrous design. And I also want you to be encouraged to believe that these small conversations are easy to face. So at the end of our time together in this book, remember how simple this process truly can be!

I hope that you feel the importance of each conversation. You cannot recreate the innocence of youth. Now is the time to begin those conversations that will lead them towards the Lord's masterful plan. As parents, I hope that this process is compelling. In this day and age sex is confusing to our children. Let's consider how the very next chapter in Genesis begins, *"Now the serpent was more crafty than any other beast of the field that the Lord God had made" (Genesis 3:1).* In our fallen world, we live with great opposition to the things most precious to God. We should be aware of the devil's schemes, but not overwhelmed by them. Our God is greater. We share the opportunity to point our children to the Creator to discover the truth and beauty of His design. We don't have to live in a state of confusion. God's word offers clear direction for our benefit.

Let's walk out these steps together, not wasting time or putting them off until the dreaded "TALK" at age 12. The time is now and the opportunity is yours to embrace. Make it simple and remember: by God's grace, you can do this!
I am so glad that you found a break in your busy schedule to read this book. As a mom, I also know that quiet moments are sometimes hard to find! So I wanted to leave you with a "cheat sheet" that can be an easy reference when you need a refresher. If you need to remember one of our five steps or more importantly, recall one of the key passages from Genesis, flip to the Cheat Sheet for a review.

It has been a joy to travel along this journey with you. Though our circumstances and geographical location may vary, one thing remains consistently the same: we are all parents who long for our children to have a God-centered perspective of sexuality. That common hope unites us as parents who are dependent on the Lord for each and every step. It is exciting to think about the Lord's redemptive plan for our children's generation. God's design is very good and your privileged role as a parent is such an important vehicle of His grace. Enjoy the ride, one simple step at a time!

CHEAT SHEET

God's Very Good Design

FIVE STEPS: OUTLINED BY GOD'S WORD FROM GENESIS

Step #1: Message

Have a plan! What is the overall image your family is giving about sex?
"Then God said, 'Let us make man in our image, after our likeness.'" Genesis 1:26

Step #2: Vocabulary

The beauty of God's gift of sexuality can be either diminished or revered by words we use. So our words must really matter!
"So God created man in his own image, in the image of God he created him; male and female he created them." Genesis 1:27

Step #3: Birth

Telling your children the story of birth will be one of the fun parts of this process! It should be a joy to teach your children about how God designed our bodies to be fruitful and multiply.
"Be fruitful and multiply." Genesis 1:28

Step #4: Reproduction

The world is your classroom. Everything you need to teach your children about the Lord and His design can be seen in His creation.
"Behold, I have given you every plant yielding seed that is on the face of all the earth,

and every tree with seed in its fruit." Genesis 1:29

Step #5: Conception

After many small conversations, you can now find yourself in a position to take this important step—talking about conception.

"Therefore, a man shall leave his father and his mother and hold fast to his wife, and they shall become one flesh." Genesis 2:24

ABOUT
Mary Flo Ridley

Since 1986, Mary Flo Ridley has encouraged and equipped parents of young children to succeed in the daunting task of starting a conversation with their children about God's design for sex.

Armed with scripture, personal stories, humor, and medical research, Mary Flo walks parents through very specific ways to answer their child's early questions with confidence. She gives parents a simple strategy that allows them to share their values along with the basic biology, and develop a positive biblical plan for introducing this subject in the preschool and early elementary years.

Through her first book and DVD series, **Simple Truths with Mary Flo Ridley,** and as a national speaker, Mary Flo gives parents the simple tools they need. Now in her second book, **God's Very Good Design**, parents can see this strategy unfold in a biblical context.

Mary Flo grew up in El Paso, Texas, and graduated from SMU. She has been joyfully married to her husband Dave for 32 years, and they have 3 grown children and 2 grandchildren...with one more on the way!